Darkness

despair

Fear Confusion

Death.

Truth

Awareness

Dreams

Growth

Healing *Humor*

Joy

Light

13   Poems and Stories

Thirteen is a prime number, mathematically indivisible.

For me it is also spiritually irreducible and emotionally magical. Somehow it wound up with a bad-boy reputation that it doesn't deserve, so I have adopted the poor waif as my luckiest number. I love black cats, too. I've always managed to find at least one willing to let me serve on staff.

These thirteen writings spanning thirty-nine years have helped me to reclaim myself. There are tools of self-discovery and healing medicine. They enable me to piece myself together and discover my shape, independent of all the shapes I have tried over the years to impose upon the original.

Following each poem is a story describing how it came to be, how I transformed it, and the ways in which it has transformed and enlarged my spirit in return.

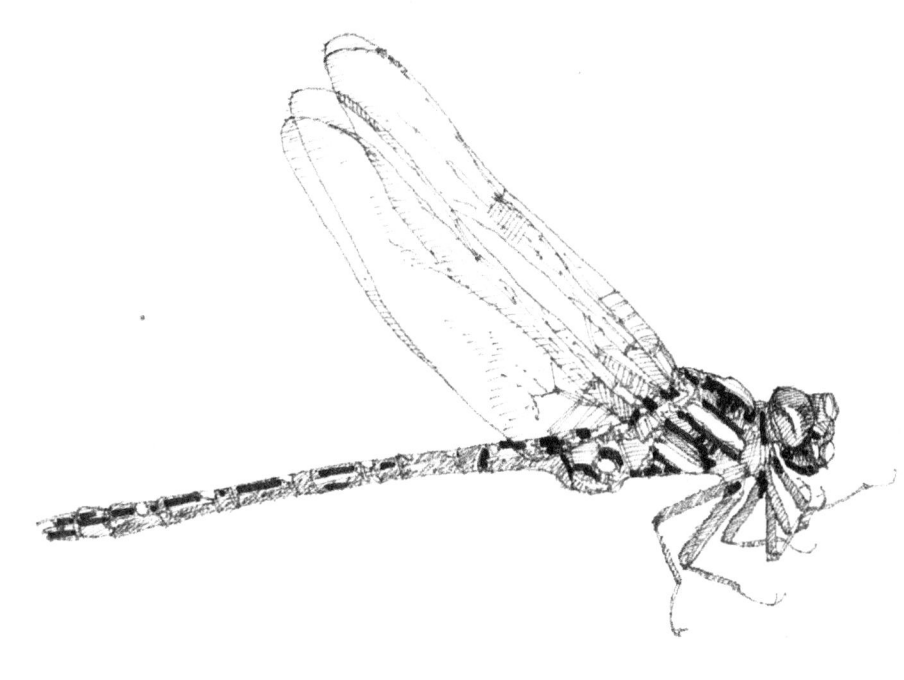

Gathering the Self

Poems of the Heart

Born on the day that All-Fools' wed Easter
Sunday, April 1, 2018

The cultivation of a sense of humor is no laughing matter.

Gathering the Self
Poems of the Heart
by David Robert Bayard

Published in-house Friday the 13 in April 2018

Copyright by Skyboy Press | Kansas City, Missouri

International Standard Book Number (ISBN) 978-0-9967380-3-3

No part may be reproduced, posted or distributed except by express permission of the author.

If it increases the level of compassion in the world, I will probably say yes.

Dragonfly art by Michael McLellin, the Nightpainter

Dragonfly Photography and Cover art by David Bayard

Front Cover: Ink on Paper

Back Cover: Spilled Merlot wine on stemmed wine glass base, ink and watercolor pencil on paper (raindrops, scene from Fantasia), refraction from crystal prism on wall, Brown Mahogany woodworking dye on paper, various pulled-up grasses, splattered KC Masterpiece Barbecue Sauce, Shingle Oak tree blossom, sticks, stems, fallen leaves, spattered mud, author's blood (don't panic, just a nosebleed), ink on paper. No beer.

Special thanks to Deborah Shouse, Wyatt Townley, Margaret Finefrock and Jennie Koenig

for their help in preparing this manuscript to greet the world

Also by David Bayard: "Sky Stories: The Sky and Nature Calendar"

Published annually since 2015. Available at www.skyboyphotos.com

Dedication

To my father, Robert Thomas Bayard, man of a different world, who in his career as a nuclear particle physicist learned to predict the course of mighty rivers, penetrate steel with his unaided mind, and leap the tall chasms of his active and fertile imagination in a single bound. And who, disguised as mild-mannered psychologist and therapist Robert T. Bayard, later fought a never-ending battle to fuse the wondrous findings of physics and science with the timeless mysteries of the human spirit.

To my mother, Jean Robert Bayard, whom I always called Jean, who loved to fling words about to find what they mean.

To my grandfather, Thomas Lucas Bayard, who passed his love of journalistic writing and photography down to me.

To my aunt Shirley Paiso Bayard, who shows me a love which shatters all puny human boundaries.

To Jon Conway, who taught me Crazy Love and not to fear the unfolding of my heart.

And to Pamela Sue Whiting, Queen of the Slipstream.

I'm done with the bushel over my light
From now on I'm hiding out here in plain sight

Gathering the Self
Poems of the Heart

Beginnings		17
1	To Cherish	23
2	Drink Me	27
3	Spring Rain	33
4	Katydids	37
5	Who Died to Make This?	43
6	Cleanliness	53
7	No Persons Were Harmed	57
8	Long Short Limerick	67
9	Simple	71
10	Home	75
11	Chrysalis	79
12	Runes	89
13	{ }	93

Beginnings

The vinyl cover of the three-ring binder had faded greatly since the last time I opened it, way back in the 1980s. It was in surprisingly good shape, having survived numberless changes during which mountains of other stuff had been lost, ruined or tossed out. But I'd held on to the binder.

I had begun writing stories and poems back then and had used the tan-colored binder to store some of the typewritten pages. Recently it caught my eye, waiting so patiently for me there on the bookshelf, and I realized the time had arrived to unearth these scribblings from my past.

I was amazed to discover I had dated and numbered each one, signed a pen-name, "windowseeker," then lovingly slid them into individual clear-plastic sleeves as if in a time capsule for my future self. As I flipped through the offerings it was like opening gifts Christmas morning.

Uncovering these ancient pages and exposing them to the light, poems penned at a time when I was beginning the process of transmuting the dirty, shameful, disgusting thing that I felt myself to be into gold, was a deeply satisfying experience. I found gold contained within them. Reading them again brought to life that different person, the "me" of many years ago.

At many periods of my life, I felt as if I had arrived at a culmination, an end, a permanent seat upon which I could rest. I had reached an understanding about myself and the world. I was done, complete. I was a cool guy now, had it all figured out and needn't go any further.

But as I look back over these dimly-recalled works, I realize

that enlightenment is not a singular event. Spectacular moments of insight and times of deep learning do occur, to be sure. But I suspect enlightenment is more of a continuum than an arrival, an odyssey which I will likely continue in perpetuity. Every time I felt finished, time and life would teach me once again that I was not.

At each moment I am walking my unique path into the mystic, as are we all, and these poems and writings are part of that journey. I look forward to watching myself unfold and finding out who I will choose to become.

I have included two of these earlier writings, "To Cherish" and "Drink Me," to begin this collection of thirteen writings. I would say "poems," but I am not quite sure what to call them, for it seems any category or genre I try to impose on them is a box out of which they will inevitably, like mischievous children, worm and wriggle their way.

My mother as a young girl put together some short writings on her manual typewriter. She called them "pomes". Perhaps she was shy about calling them poems, or perhaps like me she couldn't quite tell what they were.

So, I'll follow her example and just call these pomes—or better yet, pommes, from the French for apples.

Pommes de Coeur: Apples of the Heart.

I do know that like apples they have nourished me, and like apples they are a replacement for doctors, a do-it-yourself examination, prescription and remedy all in one. We nourish one another, me and my pommes.

Feel free to retreat to your favorite spot, let the breath slow down and share a bite.

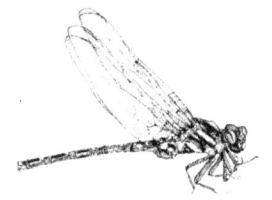 

Les Pommes

I

To Cherish

Sometimes when the blue notes come
    I'm alone on a hillock
Thrashing trees roar in a gentle wind
    with leashed power
And the small grasses repeat the movement like
    dancers on tiptoe

When the sun sets I find
    the moon was impatiently waiting for the gloom
To creep into the emptied corners
And suggest unbelievable shapes
A magical spider works at its fragile web but
No creature strong enough
    destroys it.

To Cherish

This speaks of the loneliness, confusion and despair of that time in my life as it was kneaded together with a sense of wonder at the deep beauty and healing power of the natural world.

I was tempted to edit it but resisted, because it had felt finished to me at the time. I present it as is. One of the things I have learned since then however is the impossibility of exactly mirroring a feeling, thought or experience in words. Probably the best that can be done is a facsimile that will elicit a similar response in others, but I doubt the translation from soul to word will ever be flawless. Language is too slippery.

In the line "Thrashing trees roar in a gentle wind / with leashed power," I meant to convey the powerful effects on our psyche and emotions of seemingly trivial events. As chaos theorists have discovered, small perturbations in a system can produce unexpectedly enormous consequences. And learning about nature is all about noticing the small things, those which no creature strong enough destroys.

windowseeker/February 12, 1982

2

Drink Me

Offered water lilies
Ancient as my youth, and still as calm
Like stretching cat she said
Drink me

Piston power tempered steel response, I
Said I'll take you rocketsoaring
Give you, make you, shake you
Smiling weaker now: am I not your Batman? She said
Drink me

The knees I'd wished to buckle from behind
Unvulcanized,
Through oft repeating penal scenes and tapes
And into unbelieving ears she breathed
Drink me

Crying
I am me, and won't turn back
The haunting bats be damned
I love that man so real,
Hidden in a thicket of hair, peering
So cleverly furtive 'midst the backdrop of my id

She was strong too, saying
Drink me

Come on, let me die, make me live,
Come here go away but
Don't become a fly, swaying upon warped record web
No, not with me—I'm too lonely, and
Cry with joy unlike the rest
She slapped me with her love, said come now
Drink me

Narrowly I crawl to david reeling
Dizzy
A therapeutic minute in my life
You're unfocused, fuzzy
Scary   and so very
Very much alive
Running, I am thumbing through the Yellow Pages
Looking under Hatred and Disgust
Wanting to be able to mistrust, and you
Are waiting in the want ads
Heart is in a box for me, opened in your hand
I see, and lips begin to
Drink you

Drink me

When I reread this poem, it took a while to realize that it was me who had written it and to recall the circumstances of my life back then.

This was about the struggle to understand those I was trying to love and the obstacles that stymied my efforts, specifically in attempting relationships with women. It was detective work into the ways in which they were working to love me despite my incapacity to receive and about my well-learned refusal to believe I was lovable.

The first three stanzas reflected the habitual ways I responded to invitations to intimacy with women: first, by seeing them as my mother, with me as the little boy; second, by assuming I should be a macho man, as I had been taught that all Real Men were, at least those who smoked Marlboros (alas, I was a mere two-pack-a-day unfiltered Camels guy back then); and third, by seeing intimacy, especially sexual intimacy, as deeply disgusting and a reflection of my own innate wickedness and perversity.

As to "Don't become a fly..."? I had discovered by then that I did not want a mate willing to be barefoot and pregnant in the kitchen and let me be the boss. Too boring and way too much work. I love strong women.

It was a healing act for me to write this back then. It is healing balm to reread it now.

windowseeker/February 12, 1982

3

Spring Rain

The fabric of heaven's garment is falling away, the opened robe,

The mist in gentle folds washing through the crisp wet sky.

She claps her hands together in quiet thunder and the rain answers, filtering through treetops as it falls gracefully across the hands and body of the earth's bathing form.

The steady shower wicks through the upper story, the leaves and limbs and bird's nests, flowing down along the trunk, the bark, down to the feet, the flowers, the May apples, Johnny Jump-Ups, and then into the soil where the cool clean water greets home after a long sky journey.

Dry leaves are wetted to pastel paintings by the mist as the soft sound of rustling velvet upon skin fills the air, drowning out the words I had gathered to describe. I dissolve. My roots follow moisture down to dig deep into the soft earth.

I try out my limbs for the first time, raising them heavenward to shoot my tender apple-green buds out the tips of a thousand fingers.

Spring Rain

On a long deep walk through the woods under a drizzly magical shower, this gem was to be found as a hologram within each individual raindrop. All I needed to do was open my mouth.

I have noticed in the Midwest that often after the first pop of thunder, rain will start falling, even when there are no obvious storms which could bring the two events together. The first few times I thought it was a coincidence, but I've witnessed it often enough to make me wonder: are the two things somehow whispering together? Is there some mutual magic which meteorologists have yet to discover?

It is always delightful to listen to nature's conversations, earth and sky and forest and inhabitants all sharing their gifts with one another. In this case it was enough for me just to witness, mouth agape in astonishment as the experience flowed past my lips, and to let it remain a mystery.

April 4, 2017

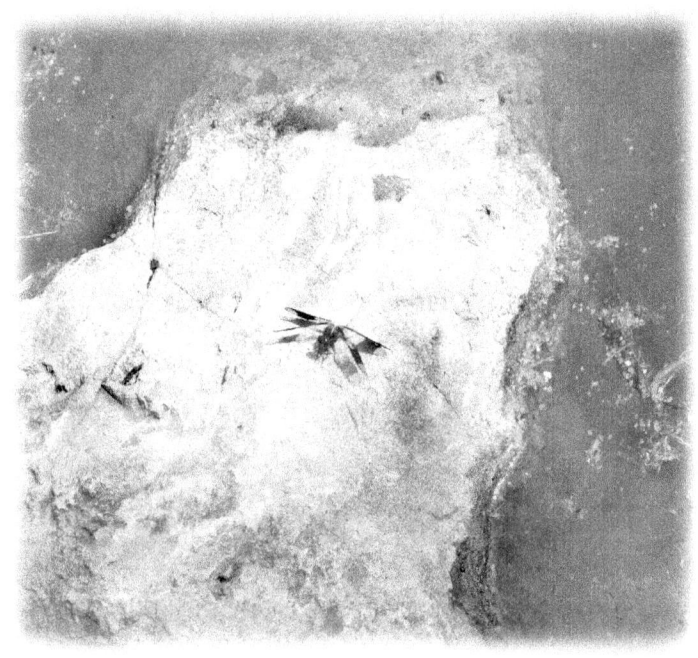

4

Katydids

Struggle bump, breathe

I carry dead katydids back to the Queen

They yet misbehave in my mandibles

Juices flow as if alive

They will not comply

Inertia! Gravity! they cry. It's the law!

Gotta work

Struggle bump

Move ahead, fall back to the very same spot.

Time. Stands. Still.

Struggle bump, breathe, struggle bump, breathe

Pull it push it pick up the dead thing living

Still pregnant with Newton's dictums

Resisting my will with its own.

I bring my gift of hard work,

Building home.

Katydids

I am a builder whose chosen medium is dead trees. I also enjoy working in a variety of other materials, though I confess I haven't yet tried to master dead katydids.

This poem, written from the point of view of the ant, illustrates the difficulty of working with dead things. Ants are pretty good at that. If they were larger and had a union, I'd consider sub-contracting the heavy tasks in my woodworking shop to them. As one of the most successful species on the planet, they've learned that even dead katydids have a bit of life yet in them. It's only fair to give it respect.

Working in the shop, I often feel as if the wood is conspiring against me—it's obeying Newton's laws of motion, as it must, but sometimes seems to be commiting willful misdemeanors. I've learned that applying brute force to an object is always self-defeating and often self-destructive. I have the band-aids to prove it.

The force which is required is upon the self, not the wood, to bend my will towards cooperating with the material, which posseses a stubborn will of its own. Dead things can yet outwit the living.

We humans tend to think of matter as inert, senseless, unliving. But quantum physics has hinted at the tantalizing possibility, through the famous double-slit experiment, that a single electron can make a choice. It can choose to be a wave. Or it can choose to be a particle.

One could think of it as intelligent sub-atomics—a smart fermion. Is that any different, except in immense spans of scale and complexity, from the choices we make? Pondering this, some scientists wonder whether consciousness isn't already imbedded within matter. I find this idea very exciting.

Some cultural traditions believe all is Spirit. They sense the life in everything around them. For them, the phrase "dumb as a rock" is meaningless; they recognize the rocks, the earth, the wood, the waters, the mountains, the sky as kindred living things. Treating them as such is the respectful as well as sensible thing to do.

People say wood is alive, and I fully agree.

In a living tree, only the outer layer of cells is alive; the inner cells die as the tree grows outward and serve only as structural support for the leaves. Wood doesn't grow on trees; it grows around them.

Once a tree is felled, all the cells are clinically dead. But you can see a record of the tree's life, back when the outer layer of cells acted as a conduit for the tree's nutrients, in the complex character of the grain. The cut wood that I use to build furniture is the tree's memory of life, day by day, year by year, ring by ring.

Some of them can remember thousands of years.

May 19, 2014

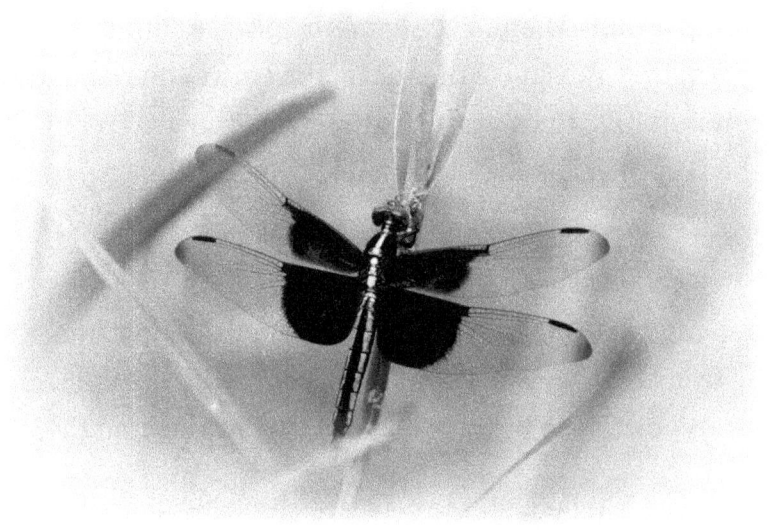

5
Who Died to Make This?

How many poets perished to bring us these pink petals fallen, spent beneath the glass vase? Who chose the voice, built their verse, sang their visions of these scant few used-up lavender limbs of lives?

How many poets does it take to screw in a light bulb? Ah, but one, though they must first set bulb aside, thread their naked body into the climbing metal spiral, spinning up till they make sparking contact with the alternating powers above to become lit up inside.

Or perhaps what was meant was to screw in*side* a light bulb. For this pleasurable pursuit most poets prefer a bit more headroom.

Back to the rose. Precisely how many feelings does it take?

The rose's beauty, hidden behind an invisible thorny defense, unattainable, sweet, bitter, gifted then gone, is a suitable enough cliché for public consumption.

But how many souls were truly transformed by witnessing this melancholia, this sacred doffing of life that brings such joyful release in dizzy-gold flecks of silky flesh spilled like confetti upon the auburn finished-oak table top? Who limned their pain properly for the future, wrote it down, contained it for those who might later notice?

Who flung their own body lifeless from the rose and slid through air to cry "I'm done, I'm spent!", alighting among these precious few pips upon the table, expiring there upon the table beneath the clear glass vase in the sunlight in the early autumn in the sunshine upon the table?

Who then pressed themselves carefully between book pages, or flung themselves carelessly into a recycling bin, or returned home to the cool moist earth to spin the tale afresh? Who mimicked nature and thereby nature became?

The roses forlorn, hovering helpless above like a team that's lost the title or has paid a price in mud and grass stains far beyond their reckoning, sense their limits. Golden colors now darkly burnished at the edges, they ready themselves for the fall to come.

Who beats this poetic vision into song, rightly plays the notes it merely hints at?

Who died to make this poem?

Who Died to Make This?

This was the gift of sitting at the kitchen table with the October sun pouring into the room, lighting a still-life of three pink roses whose blooms had started to wilt and drop their petals. I mused on what it felt like to be the doomed rose, the fallen petals.

At first writing I thought it was drivel. When I returned to it later it still felt like drivel. But each time I'd polish it up a bit, then throw it back into the drivel bucket.

No one's first work is complete but must be worked and worked, trimming away imperfections of intent and execution, rendering it into a more perfect resemblance of the artist's vision (which often as not evolves along with the creating and thus gets worked and refined itself), and boiling it down to the point where it contains nothing untrue or superfluous.

Few things spring into being full-blown like Athena from the head of Zeus. Perhaps it's in the nature of creativity that its children are ugly and misshapen when first spilling from the womb. After a long spell of letting this writing gestate, I lifted the lid of the bucket again, and lo and behold! —something was different. Maybe the writing had changed or I had, but it seemed transmuted into something not half bad.

I added some more stuff, notably the part about the light bulb (it doesn't fit, throw it out! Put it back in! Now it's a Frankenpoem! Pull it back out! It's meaningless drivel. No, it's meaningful drivel. But still drivel! Well, now I kind of like it. Well, then, throw out what you don't like. Not that one, you idiot, the other one! Now I don't like the one that's left. Yes, you do. No, I don't, I just think I'm *supposed* to like it. Don't argue with me, I know what I'm doing. No, you don't. Yes, I do! Oh, right! I forgot. We're the same guy. You know me so well.). Then I put it in the book. I hope it was worth it. If you find any more drivel, please don't tell me. It's finished.

When we are told repeatedly as children not to have feelings, not to cry, not to feel bad, not to make our parents feel bad, or worse, that *we are not experiencing what we know we are experiencing*, we learn to deaden ourselves. We learn the art of emotion-cide.

Feelings are indestructible. When we tell our body to get rid of them it simply tucks them away in a safe place deep within, a place we can no longer reach. We then lose the capacity to feel them and our inner truths become inaccessible.

But suppressed feelings erupt from time to time in ways that surprise, bewilder and frighten us, taking the form of neuroses, tics, secret longings, fears, crazy notions, and hidden shameful disturbing thoughts. They appear especially in dreams.

These outbursts are our inner selves struggling to be free, to come out into the sunshine of our consciousness and be alive again.

For me, poetry is one of the most powerful aids in unearthing my buried self. Recognizing the ugly ducklings that first spill from my pen as raw nuggets of truth that just need a bit of polishing has helped me reclaim those long-ago forgotten parts of myself. Now I can let them tell their stories. Now I can listen.

It took a while to distinguish the real from the imagined. My method these days is to ask myself: does this seem wrong or unacceptable? Do I feel bad, ashamed, a little disgusted with myself? Hmm… this is so vaguely *familiar!* I believe I've struck gold.

This poem asked me to consider what it feels like to be a dying rose imprisoned in a vase with the sunshine on its skin, bringing light which it knows will never again bring life. What it feels like to be a single slender petal sloughed off its parent flower to wither and die alone. What it feels like to be a light bulb screwed into a socket and to become turned on.

What it *feels* like to be David.

6 Cleanliness

Brave and gallant warrior of the dust cloth
   Cleansing all the spirits of the house
A flurry of activity and motion
   Though not exactly quiet as a mouse

   Watch out! All you bunnies made of dust
She'll sweep you off your feet and out the door
   No corner of the room shall you be safe in
Not the bedspread not the desktop not the floor

Against the whirling hurricane of her
   The cobwebs and the cat hairs are no match
Don't imagine you'll escape, you mess and clutter
   There's nothing out of order she won't catch

Don't stand before her idly being dirty
   For even brand-new carpets get the shakes
She will lift and polish every knick-knack
   The amazing thing is nothing ever breaks

Wow, I really wish that human cloning
   Would hurry up and finish: this I seek
So we could have a dozen of her made and maybe then
   Have two of her for each day of the week!

Cleanliness

Our cleaning lady...whoops, I've always hated that phrase for its condescension. Let's say sanitation engineer...whoa, back up, that's even worse! Then let's begin with:

Our home-purifying person is as much a part of the family as anybody. Years ago when she cleaned my wife's office, she would encounter our black cat, who was in the habit of ensconcing himself in a wicker basket on the desk and drifting into whatever meditation it is that cats meditate.

In order to clean the room she would pick him up, basket and all, set him down somewhere else while she cleaned the desk, then gently carry him back to his spot. He never once twitched a whisker.

When she leaves, everything is in place, the dust has settled into her vacuum and been carried off, and there is an ineffable feel to the house that involves all the senses. It cannot be duplicated by any application of air freshener, incense or smudge. It is a wonderful restoration of the soul.

March 29, 2018

By the way, when I asked *her* what title she used, or what she wished to be called in the book, she just said, "Oh, I'm the cleaning lady."

7

No Persons Were Harmed

No persons were harmed in the making of this poem, my dear cousin, but during our last goodbyes I leaned in through your car window to give you a hug and may have cracked a rib.

The family had gathered the night before the Eclipse. I took a grainy photo of us on the dewy grass in the deepening dusk. We laughed. Was it time played a trick on us, skillfully exchanging long for short? We laughed again. You, me, all of us were together, awaiting the morrow when the Sun would wed the Moon.

> I learned about the Solar System
> In fifth grade science class. How planets formed from rings of dust
> Revolving in their separate circles. How gravity attracted them,
> How they danced a complex pattern over time.
> How one planet's gravity could overpower, overwhelm,
> Instead of attracting fling another body out of orbit.
> Drifting pebble lost in space,
> I plunged beyond the Kuyper Belt. There was no warmth;
> I did without. No air; I breathed the vacuum.
> Staring into my mirror of ice, Narcissus,
> Whose reflection was not to be trusted,
> I grew my world within the fold of stars.

Long ago I had to withdraw for shelter against the withering clutchy things that pass for love. Now returning, leaning toward possibilities, I invited all of you to share my world again. Amazed that you accepted. Aware of what I'd missed, making up my lost

and drifting time.

Next day nature skillfully exchanged the solar eclipse for a violent tempest. Were you disappointed? I couldn't tell. We were all too busy escaping the deluge under a hammer of rain. I only know what I then discovered: the eclipse was just a good excuse to see my family. Nothing else mattered.

>I am tugged by the warm and steadfast weight of solar gravity.
>I fall into orbit among the family of inner planets.
>My icy surface melts. I cry it into joyous oceans.
>I accrete new earth upon my solid rocky core.
>I grow new life upon my outer surface. I make oxygen.
>I breathe.
>The Sun is still too bright so sister Luna blocks the pain
>That I may see the distant stars and nearby planets from my
>   rediscovered home.
>I will carry both these realms within me ever.

You were last to leave the next day, I could not bear it. Through your opened window leaning in against the rules, already two hugs and it's rude to beg a third but I need it, need to give it. Help me to discover what it is you love in me, what it is you see.

Giving a body a hug through the window glass rolled down at my tapped request, the opening squeaking goodbye hello, goodbye hello, goodbye hello.

One hug more. To cement what I think you mean, make sure of what I mean, I think, in a flurry of well-thought planning and spontaneous magic moment occurring both together, I didn't do it, it did me, nearly leaping through the driver's window, the chasm, a spasm of bright recognition on your part when you saw I was about to tilt

up my legs and pour myself through the opening across the sill like a lovesick fish to slide down embracing your body, arms wrapped round you upside down with my head resting gently strong upon the parking brake.

Body to body no secrets needed none betrayed, all loved only loved all parts loved as God intended, no bad parts no bad whole.

My rib, Adam's rib, must have slid across the window well, I didn't notice at the time but felt it as you drove off, the sharpness of bone not muscle it felt like right down to the bone, my left-side femininity bruised by risking.

Since then all has healed. I have not been harmed. But I may have cracked a rib while leaning over your side window to give you a hug when we said our last goodbyes.

Here I stood after, while there was a moment, while there was still time, while there was a still moment in time during which I sought to discover whether the cracked rib so near my heart so miraculously mended was a wound or a flower.

No Persons Were Harmed

As a young man, I ran away from home to join the circus, among other things, for a time that grew into a quarter century. It wasn't until later that I recognized what a life-saving act that had been and why I needed the distance to attach myself solidly to my own roots.

But the separation from my immediate family was also a separation from my extended family, dozens of cousins and bevies of aunts and trunkfuls of uncles, of whom I had only a few dim and distant memories from childhood. I returned to reunite myself with them as an adult. They welcomed me back without judgement and without question, arms wide. I recognized that I had always been loved by them—something I'm not sure I understood as a child—and in return I uncovered and polished the love I held for them all that time.

So when the Eclipse of 2017 was predicted to pass over Kansas City, I invited my family to share the experience at a nearby state park. We camped out the night before on a spit of land by a lake.

The eclipse itself was a bit of bust. Clouds rolled overhead and blanketed the Sun five minutes before "The Moment" occurred. They brought with them a two hour tempest, driving us like ants at a picnic to gather our stuff and scurry out of the park, along with ten thousand other Eclipse sightseers. We arrived home three hours later.

I can't speak for the others, but I wasn't disappointed. For me the experience of reuniting with family during those three days touched me more deeply than I had expected. It was enough.

When the last cousin got into her car to drive off, I felt a frantic need for one more hug. I was amazed when she hugged me back, upside down, as if it were the most normal thing of all ~ as if I deserved it. But then I am still learning the laws of true love.

August 21, 2017

8

Long Short Limerick

I struggle to pull all the drivel out of my writing
I want it to be all sharp, incisive and biting
I hope I've succeeded
I know it's sure needed
  Otherwise I'll never discover what I have to say to myself, by trying too hard to please others;
  or going off point, digressing, meandering, wasting my own time and that of whoever bothers to read it;
  or rhyming or rhythming for no reason, or making up meaningless words like rhythming just to be cute;
  or pushing the thing out the birth canal too fast;
  or trying to be famous or rich, or both, or trying not to offend, or trying to offend, or trying to keep anybody from figuring out what I'm doing;
  or preening or deigning to condescend, or being overly lofty (His Puffiness) or unduly unworthy (I'll have the worms, thank you);
  or too coy, overfamiliar, cutesy-futesy, deadly serious, humorless, or bland;
  or being too wordy or terse, or too boring (which is way much more worse!);
  or being too blunt or too squishy, or confusedly all mashy-mishy;
  or by doing anything else superfluous that doesn't lead straight to the point at the core of my being: my truth.

  Anything that doesn't carry me bodily into that realm which when stepped into rightly and listened to deeply has always been for me the very, very, very most exciting.

Long Short Limerick

A work of art is finished not when there is nothing more to add but when there is nothing left to subtract. This extended limerick portrays the work of putting that into practice.

Mark Twain is credited with having closed a letter to a friend with the apology, "If I'd had more time, I would have written you a shorter letter." Boiling writing down to thick and nutritious stew indeed takes some difficult but ultimately rewarding time.

Often, I will begin a poem with some vague Thing inside crying to come out. In the process of writing I will begin to recognize its face, feeling my way along its features, the chin, the cheeks, the eyes, the mouth, and find out what is part of the shape and what is not.

As the boiling-away continues and superfluous content is subtracted over and over, the result makes a lot more sense to the reader. But for me that's a side effect. I do it for more personal reasons. I want to get as close as possible to aligning myself with myself. I'm curious about this person that I am. The boiling, done rightly, releases the vapors of self-deception, dishonesty and sloth, heals wounds by opening them to air and light, and allows self-love and joy to percolate to the surface. After that, finding the right path is simply a matter of stepping forward.

August 27, 2017

9

Simple

Spring flower says
All we need
Why talk further?

Simple

Sometimes simpler is better.

February 2018

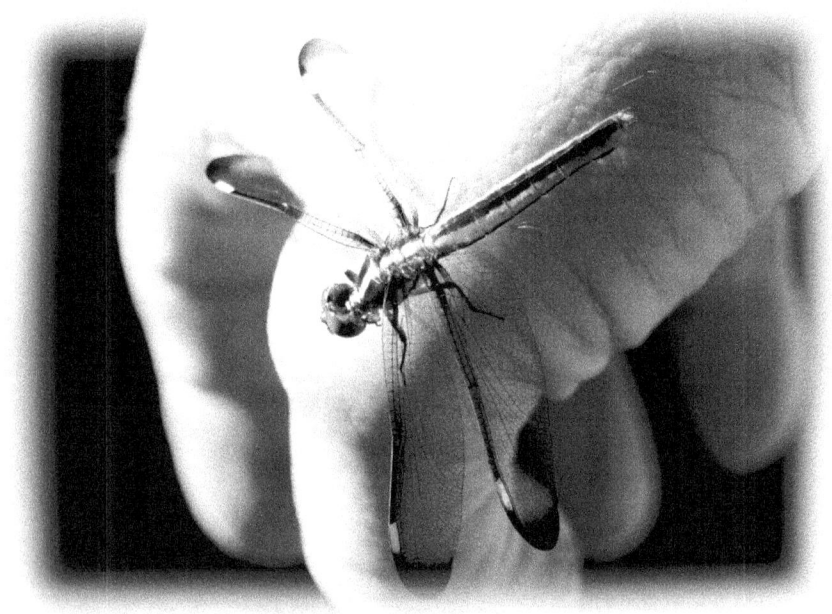

10

Home

The Body

What is
This matter of
Which I found assembled
That eats and drinks and thinks and dreams
As me?

The Dwelling

From the
Air it looks small,
When I enter, bigger
Home can swallow me and world
Welcome

The Earth

Iron
Marble sailing
Skin has burst to life
Rocks dream themselves to consciousness
Awake

The Sky

By day
Weather rules us
By night we glimpse neighbors
The sky is our window and our
Ocean

Home

This was an entry for a project called HomeWords, created by Wyatt Townley, Poet Laureate of Kansas Emerita. It was a syndicated weekly newspaper column published statewide, using poetry in a tiny form to approach a big theme: "home" from micro to macro—body, house, land, and sky. The poetic form, American Cinquain, consists of two syllables on the first line, four on the second, six on the third and eight on the fourth, with two pregnant syllables occupying the last.

The Body: I am astonished by this mechanism in which I find myself: its ability to command its own movements, to reason, to sense itself and the world, and to imagine–all from a lump of inert matter!

The Home: After a plane ride, I was struck with how the apparent size of things changes with distance. I pondered how arbitrary and tricky scale can be. How can my comparatively small home feel so spacious after that vast experience?

The Earth: How did this globe catch fire with life, creating something which could contemplate itself? I love a great mystery story.

The Sky: This is our larger view, intimate by day and infinite by night, showing us sometimes our world and at other times, others.

This was a very satisfying exercise for me. To submit to the tiny form gave me the freedom to exclude all that tried to crowd itself into my work. It forced me to my hardest task: containing myself.

April 20, 2014

II

Chrysalis

You, sir, are a
formidable opponent, sir,
You death thing you,
/
Always lurking, you are—at least if there are
Shadows. Otherwise in daylight you seem
A decent enough fellow and quite detached.
  Why do you task me so?
I never knew of you save through dim rumors
Proved soon enough untrue because Ha!
I'm still here, aren't I?
Plus, I could rock the outfit better than you with a
Scythe and a $2 beach towel.

There I go again. My ego loves to churn in
Useless rebellion, as if the love I leave behind will
Not be enough and must be augmented by
Bronze statues.

I see you there in the thicket under the fallen leaves;
Here you are ever present
In me and in the living
Branches of every tree, in the birds and the fish in the waters,
There in the flowers in the galaxies and all poetic things
As well as in those only sleeping.

I understand, I think, though I sure don't like it.
But then I am not Me, I only live in his body.
Me knows well enough that new
Horizons beckon and must be won,
And this we can only do by
Becoming the horizon.

We bloom and we ripen, then fall to our compost
Having sealed in our bodies all Summer's wisdom
So that from that earthy soil
Innocent blossoms may awaken in the Spring
With a fresh new ripeness in our old wisdom reborn.

Chrysalis

I have always wondered whether death had a purpose. I can never be sure because research on a personal level is so permanent. But I used this poem to express my confusion, curiosity, rage, anxiety, fear and awe when my Aunt Shirley Bayard was nearing the end of her life.

She passed away early this year, her dying perhaps no more harrowing than any of death's ordeals, but I hope that when I meet his jagged blade I will display half the grace, dignity and courage which she did. Surprise, denial, resistance and pain were part of her experience, too; she is only human. But she was helped by her deep faith that death as well as all of creation has a purpose.

In the months before she departed, I had spoken with her often. I would sometimes ask her to come visit us in Kansas City. At first, she demurred: "Oh, David, I don't think I would be up to the trip now, I'm too frail." But I didn't mean visit us now. I meant visit us after. I didn't have the wherewithal to explain that distinction to her at the time. Perhaps I didn't want to bring her attention to the fact of her imminent death, especially when she would drift in and out of awareness of that reality depending on the day and the hour.

But at deeper levels she must have gotten my message. Two weeks after her departure I had a vivid dream in which she appeared.

I drove through a dark tunnel, frightened and lost in blackness, to find myself in an ancient utility room. A tramway led backward and

upward from the room, though I could see that the leather sprocket chain which would have pulled my truck was broken and useless.

A soccer ball flew unexpectedly into the room. I read this as an invitation to play. I tossed it back. As I did, I glimpsed the bottom of a young girl's skirt, which I later recognized as part of the Little Bo Peep costume Shirley had worn in a school play as a child. Her shiny black shoes skittered off into a tiny doll house and a mischievous voice cried, "Tee-hee-hee!"

Suddenly I knew, or was told, or sensed—in the way of dreams—that there was a rapturous sky to behold somewhere further up the tramway shaft. I grabbed my camera and started climbing up a ladder toward the opening. At this point I became aware that I must be dreaming, and the realization snapped me into full consciousness, yet still within the dream. I raised my hands to find out what they looked like and was startled to find that my left hand had been disfigured as if in an industrial accident, the middle fingers grotesquely stubby and scarred.

I immediately recognized the connection between my hand and Shirley's left foot, which had several toes bent permanently at odd angles, not painfully so but simply misshapen. I cried out, "Oh, I get it! This is about Aunt Shirley!" and the whole dream's meaning instantly became clear. Saying this aloud in my fragile state of lucidity also jolted me into real wakefulness.

She had been letting me know in the strange yet unambiguous language of dreams that where she was going, to the place where I could not yet follow her, there were beautiful skies all the time and no

need of worry, fear, longing or loneliness. She had arrived home after her ordeal and was at peace. Her misshapen body was now as whole as it had ever been, and she was among those she loved who had preceded her through the one-way gate.

I awoke from the dream with a profound sense of wonder, a deep and unshakable joy. I knew she was alright. I knew I was alright. Thank you, Shirley Paiso Bayard. We greatly enjoyed your visit. I appreciate your mischievous playfulness and hope you find your flock of lost sheep.

I will see you soon.

October 29, 2017

12

Runes

The ancient stones portray their runes upon the gentle sand

And gather in tall tales of ships and sailors as they wash up on the tide and present themselves to land

On their weathered faces grows a wisdom which is whispered on the ceaseless winds

We could do more, they say, but all that can be pulled away is at the bottom of the sea

Think not, thou ephemeral brief skins, that they are lost, for nothing that exists is without our memory

Sing and dance upon the deck and challenge just this once supremacy, for all is hope and all is pain mixing endlessly in rhythms great and small

The cold blue sea will seize you in its warm embrace, as you cannot be lost, no matter how storm-tossed, and the end is the beginning which you never really left but still are gathered up within our sleeve

Your trials have a purpose far beyond the ones you give them, visible to those who will allow a mystery

We have watched you and have loved you and you've given back, you see. Your trick of sowing love within each other shall be gift enough for thee

There is no need to thank us or to praise us

Just to be.

Runes

I received this poem during a cool misty afternoon in the forest. I had just finished walking with Tawny, our tawny-colored dog, through the wood. Something said to me that if I were to go walk again in the dreamy vaporous rain (and bring the dog, of course), allow myself to be quiet and to be who I was without messing with myself, then this ... something... would be able to formulate and download the deep data to my hard drive.

I gathered the first few lines, walked back to the house to write them down before they vanished, then went out again to reap some more. The second or third time I did this, panic set in as I feared the words pouring in so quickly would be lost. But relaxing and slowing down allowed them to enter and remain, and they soon became embedded in memory. I felt as if a glowing message had combined itself with me.

March 29, 2018

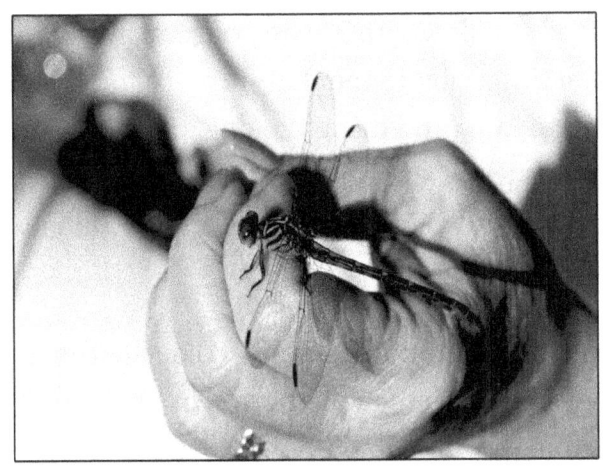

13

{ }

I am humbled before that great thing which has thus far
   roundly defeated my every effort to name it
but which I strongly suspect is identical
   to the true nature of my self.

{ }

{

}

March 2018

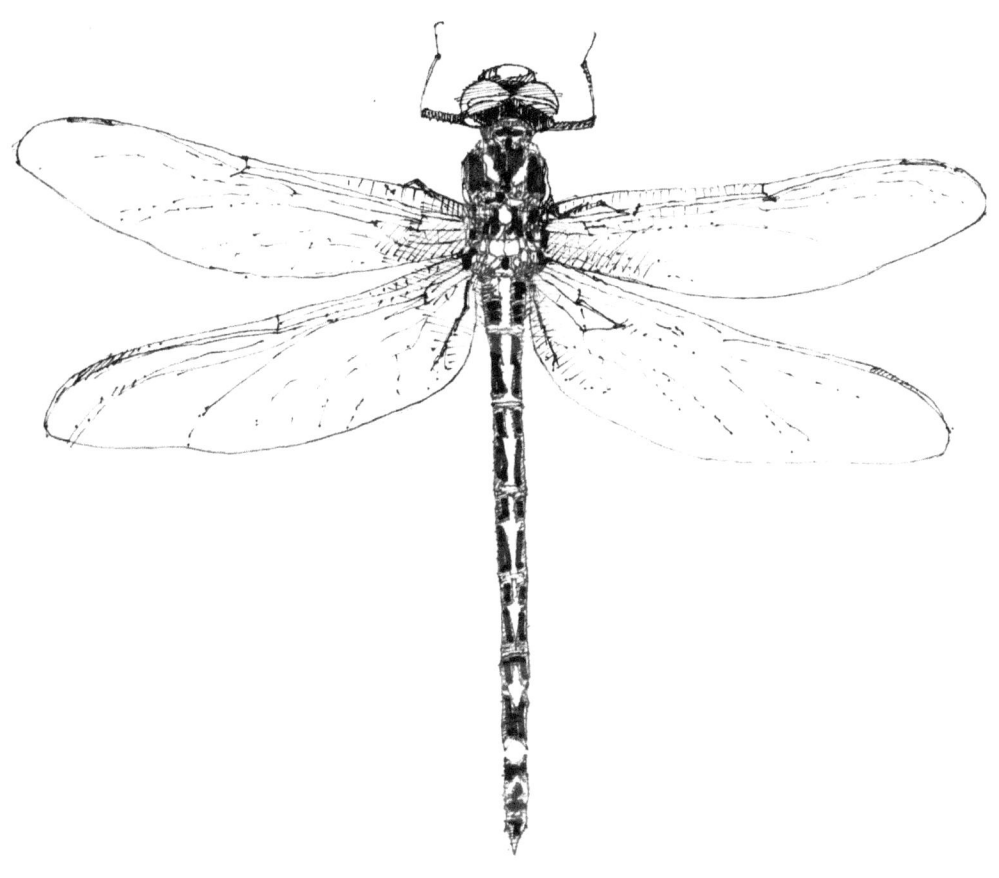

The Dragonfly

Breaker of Illusions

David Robert Thomas Bayard

dreams that he is a woodworker and photographer and that he is the owner of Samurai Woodworks, where he crafts fine custom furniture; and that he owns and operates Skyboy Photos, which makes available his photography and verse about sky, forest and nature. He fancies that he lives in Kansas City, Missouri and that he is available to the public, should you happen to be a member of that distinguished body, by telephone at (816) 765-0080 or by email at db@skyboyphotos.com .

Additionally, he imagines that he has just written his first book of pommes and that you are now holding said book in your very, very hands. He would probably be thrilled that you find it to your liking.

Please do not disturb or pinch him. Thank you.

Photo courtesy Jacqueline Giambrone

there is no need to end the mystery

                                                                   let it begin

www.ingramcontent.com/pod-product-compliance
Lightning Source LLC
Chambersburg PA
CBHW060425010526
44118CB00017B/2367